Free Verse Editions

Edited by Jon Thompson

Also by Matthew Cooperman

Books

Imago for the Fallen World

Still: of the Earth as the Ark which Does Not Move

DaZE

A Sacrificial Zinc

Chapbooks

Little Spool

Still: (to be) Perpetual

Words About James

Surge

SPOOL

Matthew Cooperman

Winner of the New Measure Poetry Prize

Parlor Press
Anderson, South Carolina
www.parlorpress.com

Parlor Press LLC, Anderson, South Carolina, 29621

Library of Congress Cataloging-in-Publication Data

Names: Cooperman, Matthew, 1964- author.
Title: Spool / Mathew Cooperman.
Description: Anderson, South Carolina : Parlor Press, [2016] | Series: Free
    Verse Editions
Identifiers: LCCN 2015044948| ISBN 9781602357440 (softcover : acid-
    free   paper) | ISBN 9781602357525 (epub) | ISBN 9781602357464
    (ibook) | ISBN 9781602357471 (kindle)
Classification: LCC PS3553.O6285 A6 2016 | DDC 811/.54--dc23
LC record available at http://lccn.loc.gov/2015044948

Cover Image: Richard Serra, "Inside Out." © 2015 Richard Serra/Artists
    Rights Society (ARS), New York. Used by permission.
Printed on acid-free paper.

Parlor Press, LLC is an independent publisher of scholarly and trade titles
in print and multimedia formats. This book is available in paperback and
ebook formats from Parlor Press on the World Wide Web at http://www.
parlorpress.com or through online and brick-and-mortar bookstores. For
submission information or to find out about Parlor Press publications,
write to Parlor Press, 3015 Brackenberry Drive, Anderson, South Carolina,
29621, or email editor@parlorpress.com.

Contents

for my three, Aby, Elias, Maya

SPOOL

If somebody doesn't fight me
I'll have to wear this armor all my life

—*Jack Spicer*

Spool 16

time is honey
and honey pain
we earn it
confusing the whip
with the watch
how it passes
year after year
a wrist with
handcuffs all alone

to ask questions
to want answers
a red balloon
caught in elms
how many times
in this life
in this life
will we stop
the honey clock

this is the
wrist to save
risk of hive

§

what someone summons
begins to stand
   moon or love
hubris   desperation   whatever
   it brings sweet
babies bloods tides
orbital longing sleeved
through lives   call
them desire scrims
rhythmic culture artifact
mining ardor between
the wars   good
benefits exchange rate
need to say
someone's watching me
I'll have another
and boom!   particular
moon goes down
making lover's pacts
with hard elements
and the soft
equivalency across borders
scales and skins
a network of
satellites children willows
we'll dare compose
      and celebrate leaps

why still it's
there pesky earth
feeling in jeans
let's take them
off and dive
dive
    dive
        die
into actual moonlight

§

a slim proposition
to be kind
wrought from life
to life   Woman
beware! this reprobate
song in silks
moon man maunders
desperately lonely   it's
     hard   it's hard
why not be
angry bored tired
these durational livers
will they ever?

to start out
sketching luminous schemes
Bali hand theater
in party shirts
the very peacock
inside us is
alone and wants
and furls banners
of leonic pride
such roars regrets
for the moon
life of planets
plummets vain glorious
resist man **resist!**

§

what color then
mute resplendent well
fitted heart whistle
noose and timber
how to talk
him down how
to brush his
hackles into eyes
clear seeing the
main of us
do not shoot
them looking and
wanting kindness so
very much wandering
sketches of him
not quite Spain
from a tower
in a coat
high caliber riffle
shoots panoptic waves
a circular brrrring!
alone to propose
this peace bullet
will eat you

Spool 20

ease and grace
and little waves
the chancing tide
around us is
a rasping timbre
a pliant heart
complexly these are
coupled hours   firebath
    and fired hearth
two a crucible
played by tongue
game and naming
what truths rise

we are foreigners
to each other
by anchors sprung
to revel shores
resemble sea bottoms
and mountain tops
say equitas madness
dove in cleft
the beginner's face
the tender's own

§

to write a
year in threes
these little wiles
and pauses   what
     they bring to
doorsteps   planets   terns
at the window
on my mind
limit is splendor
bright folds now
love or parenting
the time it
loses or looses
indelible hows plotting
the new child
the better man
bird in hand
bonus weir like
a line singing
makes a limit
out of days
slowly the dark
an imperfect finity
forever in time
these nights splendor

§

it was white
when I looked
up the sky
child of mine
remembering red a
balloon over rooftops
sitting quietly classrooms
chalk sawdust disinfectant
a clear aquarium
into the future
it was possible
a weary man
seeing a child
to inhabit moods
ask three questions
what is bearing
who are others
lives the needs
to live surreptitiously
better packages minds
to mend and
so inhabit opposites
our alter ever
simply to hymn
be other you
in that classroom
distance my strangers

§

have you seen
your hands in
dreams dark darkness
and light   a
    functional rest to
climbing thoughts   why
    let down people
and privilege glooms
these fingers strangle
thoughts of freedom
by being mine
they remain still
on the cliff
we all need
prompts records of
people I knew
I knew people
as gravity not
nostalgia but action
it seems in
a dream quite
real   the starry
atmosphere loves me
the detachment of
hands from bodies

    so hard to
    make real objects

Spool 24

our and aar
a sea encrypted
why sailor leaves
and navy persists
their fast boats
to shuttle hunger
my increment longing
how musics accrue
like the blue
dolphin street   close
    but not quite
a moon for
proximate wishes see
hover craft hovers
the line suspends
invisible traces round
parcels of sound
each package's stem
has a stern
the glow no
oar sufficiently dripped
in the drift
my breath lingers
navy deep respires
labor needs swimming
ocean to imagine

§

what myriad gypsies
jews and thieves
haunt the house
of the man
who's left standing
stock still today
with his daughter
your daughter and
the history of
arse migrations we
        move the glacier
glaze the barque
thieve and steal
a moment under
sodium street glow
the flowering thistle
our clement green
in airborne tufts
seeds say nomad
eros all kings
a budding stay
think of travelers
jews and gypsies

§

plane in sky
seen from car
driving horizon   now
    it goes down

on the news
some people spying
we're not home
a pervasive anxiety
intrudes on a
Ford Probe or
a gathering society
severs my protest
race on race
city on city
is it we're
free from the
surveillance when we
made the surveillance

I'm not saying
I'm not spying
but unconditional mind
keeps coming round
I pay attention
watch my breath
try humble enlargement
or submit accounts
the plane flies
as if unperturbed
the camera pans
inventing disaster   what
    white line descending

Spool 4

he says he
does he loves
her she's his
girl a tender
of blue ships
in surly harbor
safe when he's
with her a
whither where't thou
lost in illusion
calm of seas
traversed in toil
all paradox learning
no work and
no rest makes
pains and dulls
jack's dull   he's
    not jack   what
do you expect
you will wife
futures it's true
days daze full
flower by a
brook the sound
of plashing water
there's a rose
mole dappled lawn
trill when she's
home   it's shining
    he's her lover

§

up the mountain
on a retreat
in a state
of pineal removal
we can be
true and must
be alive so
faith is waking
the daily dose
small perfections in
not shouting "I'm
going to be
a better man . . ."

like bonus wear
the ballast under
reincarnation or pines
or joining ends
it's smoting mode
filling a sail
motion in marriage
a monster truck
        "drive," she said
"drive it fast . . ."

§

what erodes this
one act play
is more than
one face on
the master's stage
the shared value
or shared bed
is it natural
or deathly to
close the gate
a castle time
to rethink mortar
the family moat
the lonely tower
I'll starve fishes
and raises bridges
to protect one
is to project
an Other it's
pan everything or
poly hosanna   "why
    golly I'm happy
to be here
    just the same . . ."

Spool 14

some deep green
maunders in woods
brush a call
from Arden wild
man hairy and
harried   he needs
  a shadow to
hide his drive
restore good grunts
the united way
gnaw a hind
or gnash tigers
kids and suburbs
are too zoned
break a leg
or tarry bloody
the uninitiated see
a tract man
but how fail
the family without
bleeding the memory

we fall in
public all time
time lost   continents
our drift slurry
make our roles
our regnant gills
primitive happens as
matter's course   we
must survive evolve

§

who sees a
sky begin to
snow   the opening
multitude of flakes
under streetlights   all
at once one
limit releases and
another becomes   imagine
the sky's beyond

parent synapse drives
spooling out / in
the breathing thread
needles thru life

yet it's not
that very night
when snow   why
how many times
this sweet pearl
so well remembered
the quiet falling
all around sparks
how many flakes
in a life

§

vow to increase
fear to diminish
eyes and hours
as ours not
yours   it's rub
the bottle and
rattle the flowers
toil the wheel
and trouble errors

what does count
continues to count
quality or sincerity
one two three
into an infinity
that senses beauty
is gathered energy

start a fire——

move freshly into
the circle first
of all fathers
a child becomes

§

mountains are perilous
a rise fall
of ancient scales
as granite's obdurate
a grain annealed
hardened by fire
risk of other
it's the near
and far weight
to the core

care engenders lure
on approach to
the sea the
body pulls pools
child never rests
and the mountain
mountains into time
rumbles each our
risky wants   it's
    give and take
our climb redoubtable

Spool 23

like a dwelling
that resembles stone
this pebble round
with round things
yucca fox body
the maggots increase
a commerce complete
from lights above
and mountains below
the stars' hy-hydrogen
a visual ripple
a vertical lash
sharp guttural tear
    Harley ripping North
   thru thrumming sage
dusting up alluvial
thousand year powder
of river true
course this is
scrim side bedroom
window out and
in the city
creaks on cricket
strings brimming each
wing and sill
a part of
a piece of
rolling roiling stones

§

poemarium in lyria
my country undone
what shores sailed
for riches spent
or wars when
experience as wives
of places put
I meant waves
down on paper
Winesburg   Denver   Illyria
our night trail
of sonorous bread
to feed heart
and soothe head
a twelfth night
remaking all Olivia
that she sleep
in burning hours
our bright threes
we invocate and
incense word   inoculate
    hive of rushes
these are round
and makest float
a syllable by
being one is
two we count
our ventricles run
the air inclines
the poem begun

Spool 5

my flinty query
to the day
what's the day
for or against
a pressingness or
receptivity in the
glands the mounds
of shit some
elixirs of wind
lifting the pine
deer scat and
lure the jazz
out of Steller's
jeet jeet and
red squirrels nut
on high wire
prepare for winter
a spring across
snow or digging
down the query
hunger and heat
my pen moving
in the sun
the liquid ink
the blood's blood

§

to dwell in
rooms as hue
you's the one
and only complexity
keeps the dusty
corner cornered   here
   it is late
I'm so alone
and unable to
make it go
or finish finish
I only wish
the there was
got to too

you are first
on a list
list complexly these
are hours and
days oh daze
to singularize and
bind disparities please
pleas baby please
make larger space

§

moods warblers work
to be swept
the room and
sun such adventure
to be made
the kitchen hours
bees that hive
and people much
is delicate negotiating
need and want
are summons finding
sounds inside lungs
so the world
is round when
love and duty
are one grace
is within you

Spool 6

what habits solve
this weary thrush
life returns rewinds
with the bird
does not agree
with the need
my darling patience
to be daily
how we are
and aren't and
how I am
this difficult man
a gnarled me
who wants ampulacious
ideas and projects
the pi design
or clear life
grows murky in
thirst more thirst
love actually solves
by being enough
capacious stillness dust
on stars on
the near hedge
put the luggage
down I yearn
a paradox true
enough for be
enough for you

§

that we do
enter by luck
    or fate   the
scroll making rustle
let's say history
just today   a
    poem by accident
in this life
a *Thee* you
are who came
riding a bike
by my garden
who said it
would be by
planting and watching
roses are visible
make this page
glow my Hottentot
    we all have
good and bad
inside us a
sinister sister a
locket of ginger
what we spring
in dreams or
noses   a twin's
    impulse to look
up   let's hope
we are not
entombed some black
fly in white
ink   formers ladders
climbing rights   we
    can be better

§

Dearest rewinder these
times of pain
before bed please
pack a sack
and two sapphires
for son ajar
tomorrow daughter also
doctor visit will
need to be
changed   the couch
is ontologically something
remote   so elsewhere
    for dreaming   it's
late   you're gone
    I'm so alone

§

When you bounce a ball on shifting
ground it doesn't return to your hand

—Richard Serra

Spool 11

a surrogate body
speaks in flame
moving suites of
O! to air
a waterdrop darkly
leaf or tongue
brachial bird throat
resides in each
gasp of seizure
wings toward a
harmony flox field
so it goes
you go and
make a flame
a match of
*T*hees to flesh
declaration   *S*o much

    lifts the leaves
       their undersides ghost
          music or plangency

§

piles of nuts
    pools of betting
that infinity determines
clusters and aggregates
a creeping dragon
an unfleet hand
every eye's a
twin   what pearls
the vision into
riot are primes
divisible making marvels
portals leaps lyrics
plurals bent of
a parroting call
I presume sites
accept form that
you are in
twined a mind
body threshing device
harrow of germ
class struggle resides
in objects travel
walking through the
eyes hand and
the mouth feeds

to be mobile
ductile need I
cast a thread
swift a vere
vessel the load
is again unpinned

§

chuff chuff a
body engines I
say it now
my hand moves
to my mouth
quite delicately I
might add but
madness mania anxiety
middle age   it's
a piece on
Merce Cunningham in
The Times he's
still smoothly staccato
so tendon rich
a tableau his
body through the
years a bandwidth
filled with bodies
moving with heads
felicities so tactilely
dimensional they say
yes I can
so I do

§

prior to meaning
is partial to
moaning the syn
in tax is
what keeps coming
I open books
and sediments feel
some reel triple
stucco on donner
on blixen multi
colored seas braid
the invisible a
steady state of
nuthatch going through
the juniper's plosive
agency makes swoon
a tangy nexus
hearing codes nose
could be leading
the show or
pollen or mansion
to house excess
squinting I hear

"feather the load . . ."
"flense the whale . . ."

exactly some etymology
lurking in trees
author was hard
of herding he
saw vowels as
substantive pets I
like meaning but
will take moaning

Spool 10

Joe Brainard is
a dead collage
printer the point
is the making
due with pieces
Marilyn some sixteen
ripped throbbing hands
are pictures spent
truly horrible years

I went to
the woods to
see what I
could sum   why
          pieces in museums
accrue fractional value
beauty the root
his lovely lament
a fragment bridge
I love you

§

It has stopped
being a matter
of being between
texts as a
matter of being
context is everything
erasing the One
rivers tides the
idea of concrete
on the city
this fine January
shining through poplars
difference marking endures
shining is continual
   look up albedo
   attention to sun
   nets the heft

§

he wants it
to transform the
very thing changed
by addition my
subtraction I am
not home he
builds a ship
to shine off
hours they go
past the ships
becoming a past
to reflect upon
is to see
a pond not
time but distance
of transport known
a toy drags
my son years
discretely shapes of
blocks he builds
a ship so
wanting to transform

Spool 40

wall is weight
    or the eye
travels   the **lead**
in the distance
closer-than-object
appears and disappears
train or reaper
landscape   thy portion
strewn with slag

    a hand catches
only so much

but the eye
eyes whole intensities
waxing its shadow
casting its glaze
on surface rolls
and fallow fields

    —infinity tearing lead

§

to cast to
crease to fold
to roll to
bend to shorten
to twist to
dapple to shave
to crumple to
tear to chop
to cut to
mind to mold

—it is difficult
to think with
out some obsession

§

a recent problem
with lateral spread
the visual field
is work endowed
to avoid arrangement
bury the lead
the mystique of
loosening the polarities

still forces tend
weight in parts
points in series
the electrical view
allows sculptural properties
the formal bodies
oddly they announce
the mesh intention—

so much failed
simultaneously was okay
being made explicit

Spool 15

rhymes with onion
starts with what
if attacked by
a mountain lion
fight back now
consider memoir later
listen very pointed
fist or knife
your ear where
you are it's
cold or warm
the bird's flown
or hysterical   "Quiet!"
what surrounds you
    makes you go
around the cactus
practicable logic or
ass pucker fear
due south by
stars the eye
glances every night

Pleiades   memory   space…

    I tried aliens
as a circle
the clock is
more feral   see
    my claw now
begins at home

§

animal rights are
theirs alone a
plumb line of
being being here
with slavering nature
intact we are
searching sensorial swarm
make point clearly
fingertip applied why
glue won't hold
nor space last
the contractors plot
got it out
for me   a
    hammer with no
nail to pound
give me talons
to tear weakness
from their flesh

§

what's in a
word and when
is a song
of shared rutting
the very crescendo
person writing down
itching for mitochondria
place-threaded grains
    Amarillos I want
to make stand

still it goes
my flagging steel
wave of guitars
mothers   fathers   friends
catalogue of losses
and ambitions lost
my furling blows
there's no land
in vanishing woods
war is continuous
I am placeless
among empty loans
elegy sputters compensation
~~or does it~~
~~or wholeness complete~~
~~or not me~~
only you bud
of my vine

§

monkey think monkey
see no evil
do no harm
say nothing incriminating
cast no stone
but monkey is
a sly flox
and commits injury
to stable identity
it's chug rum
with fungo or
elicit an orange
the spectrum quavers
new message from
Mars a warning
there's fighting in
these fighting words
a chaos loosed
a man unplumbed

Spool 26

snow so real
it singes as
it falls both
here and dreaming
something thick like
blankets' heavy burden
on the lap
my face cold
was a ride
through north snow
some Lake Tahoe
blue parent eye
with lost ponies
skidding across asphalt
lessons learned how
real life imaginary
works a source
snowed so hard
could say we
weren't really moving
    white amniotic holocraft
    blood and nostrils...

except the bells
kept us safe
come back now
a ringing through
when I was
new of singe

§

a guardian angel
protein's been discovered
fighting cancer wherever
the man or
woman goes hospital
a tiny string
of defenses webbing
a process central
to life how
a cell responds
to stress or
perturbation in its
environment a "P
53 has an
awesome responsibility" not
fully understood the
structure of flaws
and triggers raising
inherited members just
like Aunt Tiny
who left early
her guardian angel
nonce proteinic fields
elusive codes   the
     bed near a
window   intersection Maria
and Willow   secret
     mutative letters hush
of longevity   snowing
          and not fixing

§

so many lives
looks   the genes
    of   the hair
  the hemes of
biologically inscribed goth
by the entrance
to the barn
remain very still
sift granule particularity
muttonchops and balls
~~you are welcome~~
~~you are not~~
we are known
by and for
hands free from
walking requirements   thumbs
    as identity filaments
new titanium hips
forward dancing strategies
yelp of joy
a cause of
appearances   the lies
            of the poets

Spool 7

some more new
thinking about about
and while I'm
at it on
and through the
time of conflicting
the desert asseverating
palms and dates
millennial sludge   it's
   the dredge of
city rivers a
dead muskrat wrapped
in a burkha
it is us
   in the morning's
sheen   the water's
the same where
ever you are
purl and fold
malarial or bottled
the body thirsts
the pupil dilates
seeing the sun's
everyones   it's our
   blood and cradle
it's the same

§

the pronominal spirit
resides in hides
outer membrane a
vein through fields
the inner cause
the quickening blood
it boils and
broods a next
generation   why some
are one and
others are laters
the coven works
to make it
last   our name
and futures are
caught in sluice
ingenuity flows a
tribe and glacier
the shortest path
to fro and
to is quench
what is left
might we share

§

what one needs
      in new thinking
ours   the tissues
which require reflection
post pastoral local
global self same
on a slide
in a dream
La Poudre spring
run off   the
      rack of a
   moose emerging from
the river
        a
   child ours I
have never seen
caught in the
glittering crown he
is king riding
and a kingdom
of new thinking

violet and rue
of a perpetual
sorrow   it spins
   by same principles
everyday the last
preservation of us
is thirst and
forage line for
a breathing hymn

§

to sing is
to be untied

thus make messy
our halftime adjustments
incline our silences
content our consolations
and make peace
when there was
shouting   the accusative
figure leans outward
    to be sure
effective grammar device
    to be clear
the two is
one in song
that's true of
forms being married
bride and poem
thrumming chocolate grinder

Spool 18

Avalon is what
they say about
it once you
accept the idea
of reincarnation any
thing is possible
body sampling or
sampling landscape   the
        next logical step
is bee belief
I've always been
an awe lover
a sky lover
there's my daughter
that's the butterfly
nebulae public domain
Vegas Vegas Vegas
it doesn't exist
like Cibola is
ents are next
to the girl
she is sleeping

§

things occur in
increments   half of
a zebra my
black and white
lies partial sayings
eye trouble or
egress you left
a cigarette burning
just so long
to drive there
in memory dear
make a place
by the winter
shore or residency
in Nicaragua now
two months gone
it was resilience
slurping the loon
the hooing haunting
for so long
it's been nice
to hear things
intimate aviary patter
red necked grebes
greater and lesser
frigatebirds   so many
feathers like straws
to sip time
the mounting season
it's been nice
a muddy wildebeast
hoo hee places
everywhere in real
increments things occur

§

forceful and often
dissect the yuk
the daunting task
of aversion patrol
a very real
person enjoined to
slime these games
of percept and
affect the outcome
make 'em pay
lawyer who hears
soprano who sings
experiments in texture
languaged to roost
rights or spectrums
a rude roshambeau
high energy cartoons
ping and strange
trace vespers still
the starlings debate
the startling debate
is what you
would do with
total control ban
lobbyists rhet talk
charlatan brill we
keep on coming
despite our lust
pirouettes and extensions
pole dancing   Bam!
a lawyer gavels
soils his creed
some honesty honestly
fleecing country sheep

Spool 22

what's speech's ring
in virtual ears
that repetition recounts
sincerity makes peace

fulsome gestures so
much human voice
making cotton rise
to recognition   "Hello?"
    I am hallucinating

I know I've
met you some
where or wearing
space and days

rhyme you say
a true blue
next life think

*to sing is
to be untied*

§

kind of crown
to wear away
my ablative unmaking
more and more
the day makes
clear the day's
a separate mass
I must enter
at all costs
the very thorn
like locust moved
a tree for
all my wandering
and a marker
king of leaves
chemicals are thoughts
quite real 'tings
not nosely separate
these lemon rinds
of material tart
my ego bloosing

§

branches prompt look

at security sky

the red balloon

a border knows

what emits carbon

your lucky numbers

for centuries puff

a physician's credo

do no harm

that hasn't changed

someone's mind is

a terrible thing

waste matter ensures

worm will go

on and on

witness was questionable

so we did

§

    permeable boundaries are
    where immigrants thrive

with concern there
and fence evocations
confront you who
and where from
in the scheme
of things are

     exits like conduits
     accelerate the phenotype
     we are more
     or less immigrants
     thrice removed we

   discovered our tombs
   to be gardens
   rimmed by blocks
   living testaments or
   sweet flag tenements

the laundry snaps
these living signs
a lively debate
about forgetting remember
your lost trace
my living grave

Spool 9

upon their eyes
their ears the
sense record so
full of taste
and touch too
a finger recoils
spells out smells
the conductor translates
makes larger space

a place for
listening is a
plot for making
this cold November
nearly gone but
not forgotten I'll
just bone home

now a larger
faculty help me
chime in refracted
waves ways articles
of speech I
say it   **"blue!"**
before the witness
letters mind mapping
days mine blend

§

tweet tweet the
vireo both here
and after   the
    sound is the
truck backing up

using the same
vocabulary is how
a verb list
or verb lists
            dangerous heel on
            the running sea
making sound monumental

to drift to
maunder to pitch

            the animal is
            in the material

§

vertigo   that's intentional

time is honey

and honey pain

is everything the

same is everything

the same is

§

of tension of
lists of Serra's
gravity and entropy
of grouping of
layering of felting
of equilibrium of
heat of ionization
of friction of
carbonization of tides

the arcs are
running slow tonight

"Evolve!"   he says
and he does

§

Because she is in a body sometimes it makes decisions
—*Mei Mei Berssenbrugge*

Spool 13

ever to fall
and never rest
rest in vowels
the wide **O**
the bird **O**
of her throat

years go by
not as catches
but as drones
autism is other
an other bird
the plan devours
speech and sleep
or sudden joy
and late weeping

biographical threes betray
the bird which
had so much
verve in its
throat   sang lark
of days or
giddy sex shop
old town tune
moved to the
suburbs risible suburbs
circling drones these
families and shrieks
of dog lovers

§

blue finchy flutter
in her eyes
wing more real
than questions all
is asking and
receiving   I long
to fly and
can't stitch ends
such so and
so my tongue
responds   its ruth
    a savage silence

the falling snow
crystal fast oaks
all toils the
world's quick spindle
turns coriolis hairwise

    family linkage nest––

    it's confronting what
I don't know
what I do
    for one planet
only one experiment

§

theories of tension
massive enclosures of
intimate space like

little wax combs
or girl bedrooms
hexagonal patterns spun
onto fresh silicon

hive rives high
to the low

a family is
a thing a
made thing almost
a true wall
we made this
thing true wall

§

render sketch   it's
   all too much
I am too
tired riding rowing
my vacant oar
heart muscle ear
hears joyous grievous
wound   inexhaustible   fluttering

what slacks there
mid winter lull
not enough to
simply be and
see Love arrive
with snow shovel

a soluble vroom
of give   I
   take it now
render sketch again
a heartsore scene

Spool 41

structure is strange
a hollow ground

symbiosis isn't the
half of it

harmony is out
cooperation is in

might we share
the family bin

the mesh made
of insubstantial stuff

anodyne of mist
only the dimness

in which suggestion
can rise *res*

§

awake   half awake

so little happens
in this life
what changes really
in her eyes

a ring wrung
to dream   a
face   a recognition

her skin's seething
difference   sweet evidence
   can't reach ends

looms a you
I choose and
you I choose

Spool 25

my faith is
stored in the
wild domesticity of
sunflowers aphids wives
how they reach
and attend faith
by being itself
an action moving
to the sun
its bright target
to point alive
the ravened leaf
by the ravening
eye my Green
sun being swan
I am beginning
to see and
continuing to see

§

to be concerned
for things rare
and daily means
to care for
them   a privacy
of surfaces faces
this body mark
of daily feed
a letter there
a G tube

these are worries
not mapped out
a concrete figure
materializes in din
a hole in
the body   her
body a hole

O fear cherish
a night swing
fit oneself to
oneself a reifying
glove like action
like anxiety too
to be concerned
for things rare
relays of force
needle in needle
her speech mine

§

she does not
speak   she does
not even eat

days are clear
but nights are
dark dark night
of the soul
when Daughter thumps
and thrashes   I
    gnash too her
future full of
~~not here so~~
a silence dozing
linguistic film   so
    thoughts bloom in
a second sight
my limited time
or timeless disposition

*P*syche drain me
apostrophize all shadow
I know not
where she goes
or how to
go to her
with articulate grace
her darkness visible
so I see
can name it
patience please please
dark dark understanding

§

and soul clap
hands and sing
and louder sing
this vowel lust
    spool it off—

time is domestic
its velocity quarks
a total cosmic

centrifugal my little
girl's girl her
wavering eyes and
watery calm this
soul side climax
wants to clap
she and me
a raveling spore
in every darkness
a visible calm
our rhizome ring
in the dust

Spool 32

some particular worm
has a mind
to mine the
frozen midnight frost
3 am and
I'm lying again
about knowing shit
from species so
like my mother
or my father
trying daily to
fit the routine
into the ring
being part of
and apart from
truly bereft is
days and nights
sleep and sanity
the distance between
you and me
she and we
sensation and names
what I calls
the terleu effect
it's terleu cheep
seeds of restless
mind to know
thy aggregate flock
between the thyme
and the street

§

feeling the shame
an other father
so fresh as
what was said
and done undone
pointed at laughed
her breached skin
of sufferings feelings
what is unknown
the daily isolations
the daily immolations
a flensed life
to whale home
my shore my
speech and future
for her thimbled
out of step

what will do
to make you
soothe her spool

§

in the ambit
of the elect
his steel wings
because she moves
becomes the radiant
bed of matter
coppice of laurel
echo of thunder
all this lists
to give names
names are gambit
trebling spurs like
life on spectrum
imagine the wind
big snowy river
a melancholy dream
of roughly ways
the world says
welcome bright auger
steel as nouns

§

he and she
a plural verity
death's tricky plinth
we give ourselves
the knife and
the car wheel
torn from hand
to mouth goes
the cry and
one more gone
an inch by
inching imminent grave

a ladder lament
sirens of daybreak
fence of slate
the smell of
burnt rubber   it's
history's random cull
the knife and
the cart wheel
the fool and
the train wreck
death's tricky plinth
for he's she's

       we are watching

Spool 33

fiery pronouns strict
unbecoming of his
definitions true agency
a true color
is a figure
of an **O**
that's all you

is what he
wants so much
he wakes wants
to throw her
into air loops
and arabesques of
what is "natural"

naturally occurring **O**
of the mouth
opening this laurel
too is violent
with his longing

§

against the animal
what minute measure
to double say
to say for
a cipher's tongue
what thread's missing

this goes on
inside a skull
a pull a
tear a daughter

language tree a
stare a bang
a hand to
stop her beating

beating heart and
beating brain this
bird brain line
to unstitch harm

the glowing weft
of right left
hemispheres in the
hive cosmic struggle
a thing unraveled

my terror there
her grinding day
I will my
star pull into
her girl nest

Spool 17

ardors are we
or sudden crimes
we set for
those we love
and perfect strangers
perfect in their
kingdoms these sharp
curves needs are
partial difficult unresolved
two hands paired
or what we
see driving there
is what we
get through arrival
being limit three
times two is
six and so
on neural bloom
releases as we
live we are
so brief in
being   I dream
    a car backwards
anneal all twists
love like a
traveller and a
wish to turn
clearly now the
road addressed you
are more numbered
great sweet wheel

§

grass from grasan
young shoots sprout
the verbal world
glows at edges
of hedges   grama
like shears or
finches fierce fall
the attractions come
out   they come
out from words

so reverse flow
weave acrostic kindness
elicit the descriptions
in connected strands
vinc penkas spingos
aby elias maya
matthew naming names

lathe of time
lave of shine
the jewel is
a thunderbolt in
the lotus void

Spool 37

alphabet begin a
hymn for grieving
or for Anselm
across the yard
or blank universe
a spelling distress
to make miracles
type it distrust
of the sea
a dark effulgence

the bird goes
down she goes
down at sea
no halcyon weaver
nor kingfisher cry
an empty nest
nonetheless to hive

and again jewel
flashes the void
is the violent
hum of action

—it was Actium
and they lived

§

an ending or
a pause   admit
the tape is
broken now so
sick and slck
the master's gone
astray   dove flew
   the hub's askew

a wager's lost
that love things
last or don't
they grind the
wife and husband
with their teeth

fragments curry favor
that's occasional sauce
to lubricate losses
or quell complaints

it's what I
thinks or gots
to give graces

Spool 21

O for wishes
to genie bottles
O for circles
around the moat

accept the small
creature awake at
the heart of
the heart poem

> *And he woke*
> *fully clothed in*
> *his bed   he*
> *remembered only one*
> *thing   the birds*

§

too much fire
too much rust
wall or comb
the collapsing home
all of it
the fire reflection
on the stick
that's tending it

why to be
a child may
mean more than
was first thought

to live in
each other's death
and die in
each other's life

> *a bird came*
> *down the walk*
> *he did not*
> *know I saw*

§

betwixt the torus
and the sphere
a matter of time
grows rust on
Cor-Ten steel

we wake every
day are awake

§

bar and rebar
again and again
wall wills stability
they are made

what protects hides
what supports leans
what grounds turns
what sites sunders

to see her
leaning there in
a rust augur
afternoon sunlight so
whole body touch
steel a surface
through molten gravity

to rend to
sew to mend
to sever heal

Spool 30

our darknesses our
canyons still a
fire in the
pines   they are
     awake   work their
color to each
tip a needle
visible green thread
of increments serializing
the furies so
in the river
on the bank
plash and furrow
our standing still
ideas in things
catch fire now
current between you
and me   rivers
changes enlarges all
feels the sear
to the tips

§

the Loved is
the court of
Time how we
pass it together
or so Alone
I want pure
Being next to
on top of
too so In
about our breathing
as I want
Space around me
to see and
talk to World
the loved Is
and you Are
most to me
here in it
let it Be
Let it be
our new house
is a Home
for the Loved
our court elations
decisions You Me

§

we lie beneath
all the stars
all the light
all the time
ever traveling beams
of eternities spelling
the speed of
what is possible
in this turn
evening's bright band
a crimson sash
to wear upon
the garment body
infinity's light as
the world without
and up or
down a standing
vessel reporting love
sixth and main
our short span
they all glimmer
report of suns
bearing plural planets
each of us
cell bright star
that other border
red sash run
our blue life
we lie beneath

Spool 31

fair no more
the heart of
the son whose
time has run
what reasons clocks
for or against
this line by
line accounting as
failure days are
brilliant figures death
a glittering timbrel
a tumbler's thirst
what alkaline water
or too casual
drink to health

and let us
live it truly
for all the
gilded patchwork so
the earth is
a summer's sun
in migrant lines
from plane's fields
repeating swath gone
song I love
you love thy
wages worldly task
one small sun
to run and
come to dust

§

is it tide
or wheel or
well of life

is it praise
or hours or
shadow of dearth

is it path
or anvil or
arrow of time

is it sense
of nothingness to
discharge the removes

a worm and
finger of one's
own black brand

death is imminent
a for me
and to me

containing the well
tightening the wheel
my single worm

to be determinate
immortal thing with
a black line

§

what the eye
must train to
see in diminishing
light takes on
the inner imprint
blood colored hyacinth

part enigma part
body that obliterates
verses were the
murex that dyed
all existence purple

all futures sound
of this casting
form   real arias
naked foundry wakefulness

§

and gear ourselves
into what carpentry
of the whirl

wood where ever
you have been
are being   time
    a single grain

magic of correspondence
        a cellar's rank
    for a steeple
word for wood
a conscious thimble

these glittering chains
run the machines
hours of public
and private speech
a tumbrel shaken
not a tambourine

now what will
I will you
the treadle and
the spool

Notes

Spool 20 is in conversation with Aby Kaupang's poem "Ease and Grace," *Absence is Such a Transparent House*, Tebot Bach, 2011. It is also sampled in my poem "Still: Ampulacious," from *Still: of the Earth as the Ark which Does Not Move*, Counterpath Press, 2011.

Spool 4 riffs on Gerard Manley Hopkins' "Pied Beauty."

Spool 23 is in conversation with Shakespeare's *Twelfth Night*.

Spool 11 owes a debt of reading to Steve McCaffery's book *Prior to Meaning: The Protosemantic and Poetics*, Northwestern University Press, 2001.

Spool 10, "he wants it/to transform," is for Elias Kaupang

Spool 40, quotes, in italics, and makes use of Richard Serra's "Verb List, 1967-8," *Writings, Interviews*, University of Chicago Press, 1994.

Spool 7 and Spool 22, quote, in italics, "to sing is/to be untied," John Taggart, "Rhythm and Blues Singer," *Pastorelles*, Flood Editions, 2004.

Spool 7 also riffs off of Robert Bly's poem "Things to Think," *Morning Poems*, Harper Perennial, 1997.

Spool 18 owes a debt of long friendship to Gregg Lauer, astral cowboy.

Spool 9 is inspired by the music of Evelyn Glennie; the genetive lists are from Richard Serra, "Verb List, 1967-8."

Spool 13 plays off of Robert Duncan's poem "The Years as Catches," *The Years as Catches: First Poems*, Oyez, 1966.; it also quotes from E.O. Wilson, in italics, "for one planet/only one experiment," *Consilience*, Vintage, 1998.

Spool 41 is in conversation with Timothy Morton's *The Ecological Thought*, Harvard University Press, 2010.

Spool 25 owes a debt of reading to Milton's *Paradise Lost*, Yeats' "Sailing to Byzantium" & Don Revell's *The Art of Attention: A Poet's Eye*, Graywolf Press, 2007.

Spool 17 is for Sue VanSchoonhoven, 1972-2008.

Spool 37 is for Anselm Hollo, 1934-2013.

Spool 21 quotes, in italics, a strand of Charles Olson's "The Kingfishers," *The Distances*, Grove Press, 1960, and a strand of Emily Dickinson's "328." It also makes use of Richard Serra's sculpture *Betwixt the Torus and the Sphere*, as well as his "Verb List, 1967-8."

Spool 30 & 31 are indebted to the philosophy of Alphonso Lingis; **Spool** 31 owes a debt of reading to Shakespeare's *Cymbeline* & Andrew Marvell's "To His Coy Mistress."

Acknowledgments

Spool was composed beginning Jan 10, 2006, in Mazatlan, Mexico, and completed on November 15, 2015, in Fort Collins, Colorado. Grateful acknowledgement is due to the following publications and editors, where these poems, or versions thereof, were first published:

"Spool 16," & "Spool 24," *The Laurel Review*

"Spool 20," *Reconfigurations*

"Spool 4," *Drunken Boat*

"Spool 14," *Free Verse*

"Spool 17," & "Spool 23," *Center*

"Spool 6," *Many Mountains Moving*

"Spool 11," *Gutcult*

"Spool 15," & "Spool 18," *Little Red Leaves*

"Spool 26," *Connotation Press*

"Spool 7," *Electronic Poetry Review*

"Spool 22," "what's speech's ring," & "kind of crown," *Parcel*; "branches prompt look," & "permeable boundaries are," *Sugar House Review*

"Spool 9," *Denver Quarterly*

"Spool 19," *Basalt*

"Spool 25," *Boston Review*

"Spool 31," *Lumn*

Parts of "Spool 5," & "Spool 20" appeared in my book *Still: of the Earth as the Ark which Does Not Move*, Counterpath Press, 2011.

More specific thanks to the following poets and editors who have helped shape the work:

Kazim Ali, David Axelrod, David Barratier, Dan Beachy-Quick, Victoria Brockmeier, Julie Carr, J'Lyn Chapman, Brian Clements, Richard Deming, Debra DiBlasi, Timothy Donnelly, Julia Dresher, Camille Dungy, John Gallaher, Gordon Hadfield, Brian Henry, John Hoppenthaler, H. L. Hix, W. Scott Howard, John Kinsella, Christopher Kondrich, Jeffrey Lee, Charlie Malone, CJ Martin, Michael McLane, Eric Magrane, Wayne Miller, D.A. Powell, Patrick Pritchett, Kevin Prufer, Tim Roberts, Andrea Rexillius, Don Selby, Heidi Lynn Staples, Sasha Steensen, Chad Sweeney, Catherine Taylor, Truong Tran, Andy Touhy, Jody Veron, and Sam Witt.

A string of gratitudes to Richard Serra, hovering "architect" of the Spool design; John Taggart, whose poetry and correspondence have pushed my idea of limit for many years; and Logan Burns, especially deep-dear reader, who nudged Spool past the limit. To Rae Armantrout, Pam Rehm, Jonathan Skinner, blurb faith; to Ann Gill, Louann Reid, Bruce Ronda, fearless CSU leaders; to my amazing under/graduate writing students at CSU; and to my collaborator there, Marius Lehene, naroc! A tremendous thanks to Jon Thompson for hearing this manuscript's straining tape, and to David Blakesley for making it beautifully happen. And a deepest bow to my poet love/love poet, Aby Kaupang.

About the Author

A former Provincetown Fellow, Matthew Cooperman is the author of, most recently, the text + image collaboration *Imago for the Fallen World*, w/Marius Lehene (Jaded Ibis Press, 2013), as well as *Still: of the Earth as the Ark which Does Not Move* (Counterpath Press, 2011), *DaZE* (Salt Publishing Ltd., 2006) and *A Sacrificial Zinc* (Pleiades/LSU, 2001), winner of the Lena-Miles Wever Todd Prize. Four chapbooks exist in addition, including *Little Spool*, winner of the 2014 Pavement Saw Chapbook Prize. A founding editor of *Quarter After Eight*, and co-poetry editor of *Colorado Review*, Cooperman teaches at Colorado State University. He lives in Fort Collins with his wife, the poet Aby Kaupang, and their two children. More information can be found at www.matthewcooperman.com.

Photograph of the author by Aby Kaupang.
Used by permission.

Free Verse Editions

Edited by Jon Thompson

13 ways of happily by Emily Carr
Between the Twilight and the Sky by Jennie Neighbors
Blood Orbits by Ger Killeen
The Bodies by Chris Sindt
The Book of Isaac by Aidan Semmens
Canticle of the Night Path by Jennifer Atkinson
Child in the Road by Cindy Savett
Condominium of the Flesh by Valerio Magrelli, trans. by Clarissa Botsford
Contrapuntal by Christopher Kondrich
Country Album by James Capozzi
The Curiosities by Brittany Perham
Current by Lisa Fishman
Dismantling the Angel by Eric Pankey
Divination Machine by F. Daniel Rzicznek
Erros by Morgan Lucas Schuldt
The Forever Notes by Ethel Rackin
The Flying House by Dawn-Michelle Baude
Instances: Selected Poems by Jeongrye Choi, translated by Brenda Hillman,
    Wayne de Fremery, & Jeongrye Choi
The Magnetic Brackets by Jesús Losada, translated by Michael Smith & Luis
    Ingelmo
A Map of Faring by Peter Riley
No Shape Bends the River So Long by Monica Berlin & Beth Marzoni
Pilgrimly by Siobhán Scarry
Physis by Nicolas Pesque, translated by Cole Swensen
Poems from above the Hill & Selected Work by Ashur Etwebi, translated by
    Brenda Hillman & Diallah Haidar
The Prison Poems by Miguel Hernández, translated by Michael Smith
Puppet Wardrobe by Daniel Tiffany
Quarry by Carolyn Guinzio
remanence by Boyer Rickel
Signs Following by Ger Killeen
Split the Crow by Sarah Sousa
Spine by Carolyn Guinzio
Spool by Matthew Cooperman
Summoned by Guillevic, translated by Monique Chefdor & Stella Harvey
Sunshine Wound by L. S. Klatt
These Beautiful Limits by Thomas Lisk

www.ingramcontent.com/pod-product-compliance
Lightning Source LLC
Chambersburg PA
CBHW022032090426
42741CB00007B/1036